Welcome Home™

Debbie Mumm

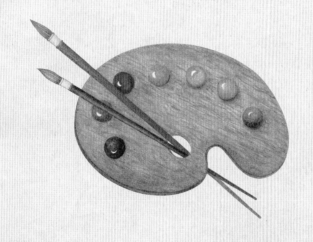

WELCOME HOME™
DEBBIE MUMM

copyright © 1998 by Landauer Corporation

This book was designed and produced by Landauer Books
A division of Landauer Corporation
12251 Maffitt Road, Cumming, Iowa 50061

President: Jeramy Lanigan Landauer
Vice President: Becky Johnston
Editor-in--Chief: Marjon Schaefer
Art Director: Tracy DeVenney
Managing Editor: Marlene Hemberger Heuertz
Graphic Designer: Shelton Design Studios, Inc.
Contributing Editor: Candace Ord Manroe
Associate Editor: Sarah Reid
Calligrapher: Cheryl O. Adams
Photographers: Craig Anderson, Amy Cooper

Published by Martingale & Company
PO Box 118, Bothell, WA 98041-0118 USA

This book is printed on acid-free paper.
Printed in Hong Kong 10 9 8 7 6 5 4 3 2 1

Library of Congress Cataloging-in-Publication Data
Mumm, Debbie, 1956-
Welcome Home / Debbie Mumm
p.   cm.
Includes index.
ISBN 1-56477-235-7 (hardcover)
1. Handicraft. 2. House furnishings. 3. Interior decoration.
I. Title
TT157.M79 1998
746.5--dc21   98-20263
CIP

WELCOME HOME™

DEBBIE MUMM

Edited by Marjon Schaefer

CONTENTS

WELCOME TO MY HOME 9

Debbie Mumm's personal tour of her enchanting and spacious two-story home provides a wealth of ideas for making a house a home.

MY BASEMENT STUDIO 10

For Debbie, the best ideas come from within. The cozy atmosphere in her basement studio stirs the creative embers even more.

THE BIRD BATH 22

Any space in the home—even the basement bathroom—can display cottage charm. Even a folk-art blackbird enjoys roosting here!

VINTAGE VOGUE 30

Sophisticated comfort prevails in Debbie's living room. Pastels—especially pinks—mix with pale, faded greens for a look that's vintage vogue.

DINING ROOM 36

The spring-fresh garden ambience that wends its way throughout the home also lends a hand in making the dining room eminently livable.

FAMILY ROOM 44

Home for the holidays takes on special meaning when Debbie fills her family room with favorite images such as Santas and snowmen.

INTRODUCTION

Debbie Mumm's designs first captivated quilters back in 1982. I became acquainted with Debbie's work when she taught at a quilt shop named Fiddlesticks, in Yakima, Washington. I followed Debbie's rise to fame at each Quilt Market, where her displays and pattern covers told me that here was a soul sister who enjoyed decorating.

Our first project together was in 1995 when Debbie graciously allowed her home to be photographed for my book, Decorate with Quilts and Collections. During the photo session, Debbie and I eagerly shared design ideas, new trends, and locations of favorite shops for the home. I totally enjoyed her 'Vintage Vogue' look and knew that Debbie's entire house had to be featured in a book of its own. So now country enthusiasts the world over can share Debbie's ideas and inspiration for a 'Welcome Home.'

Nancy J. Martin

WELCOME TO MY HOME

I loved doing this book. It feels very personal to me to share my home, my art, my studio, and my special treasures with you. I hope you not only find inspiration for creating your own beautiful home, but also an opportunity for us to get to know each other better.

Because it's so important to me, it's fun to share the side of me that you don't see through my country-quilt designs. I love to integrate different looks in one room—you can't deny the country undertones in any of my rooms. I enjoy creating a nostalgic feel and collecting things that bring you back to a time when everything was made with a lot of detail and craftsmanship. There's actually nothing authentic about the room styles or periods, other than it's all authentically 'me.' Nearly every room has a different look and theme. I really appreciate and enjoy the visual stimulation of a variety of different looks and colors. I'd get bored if it was the same look throughout—my home has become a very personal extension of who I am and what I love.

My bedroom shows the greatest fusion of styles—classic architectural details combined with country—I call it 'Renaissance Country.' I absolutely love this room and, many evenings, spend hours there, studying the magazines, catalogs, and books that arrive in the mail each day. Also, the special friendship quilt on my bed, signed by friends, family, and neighbors, keeps me warm and gives me comfort.

I rely a great deal on a group of artisans who have done a lot of work for me in my home. I articulate my vision of what a room is to be and then work closely with them throughout the process. I love to collaborate with other creative people and I love having so many pairs of hands.

Shopping certainly has become one of my most favorite hobbies. Not only do I enjoy it, it is also a big part of my research and development process. It's stimulating to look at color, design, style, and trends. My favorite places to shop for ideas and inspiration include antiques shops and shows, interior design stores, unfinished furniture stores, gift and consignment stores, and nurseries.

Furniture and accessory recycling turns the ordinary into unique. You'll see several samples of this throughout the book. Sometimes I like a piece of furniture or accessory, but I'm not attracted to its finish. Paint it, crackle or spatter it, and antique it.

I hope a smile will come across your face as you see some of the fantasy environments I've created and that you will enjoy making the connections between my artwork and my home. "Decorating isn't for whimps!"

Debbie Mumm

MY BASEMENT STUDIO

When it's time to nurture the roots of creativity—or a garden's worth of plants—Debbie heads underground. Her basement studio is abloom with fresh ideas and living color.

My Basement Studio

O ther folks may head for the high ground to get their inspiration. But for Debbie, the best ideas come from within. That's why snuggling down to business in her basement studio—a metaphor for going deeper within herself—makes such good sense. And, thanks to some of her most personal decorating, the cozy atmosphere that awaits her there stirs the creative embers even more.

Faced in brick that she's painted to highlight the hearth in her signature black and ivory, a fireplace wall bears a treasure trove of earthy textures and treasures. The garden theme that appears on much of her work resonates clearly, starting with an antique potting bench. Garden accoutrements are plopped on and against it like long-time friends. An old wooden rake and a painted trellis flank the ends. Time-worn metal watering cans, clay pots, and plants-in-progress are scattered on the shelves. Favorite folk-art—an assortment of birdhouses and beehives—are focal points that Debbie's fans will recognize from her work.

14

Comfort, contrasting colors, and coziness are recurring themes in Debbie's art. Little wonder these same elements appear again in the design of her basement's conversation/sitting area. Mounted behind the sofa as art, one of Debbie's quilts sets the area's palette and mood. The quilt's contrasting palette, of bumblebee yellow and black with tan accents, repeats on the geometric-patterned fabrics on the sofa. A cache of cushy decorative throw pillows picks up the colors, but on different fabrics for casual ease. A contemporary black lamp steadies the design with simplicity.

With its shingled roof and two-story dwelling, this painted birdhouse is a source of delight to Debbie, who surrounds herself with favorite objects that often become incorporated into her works of art.

IF YOU LISTEN WITH IMAGINATION, THE BUZZING OF BEES CAN BE HEARD IN THIS YELLOW-AND-BLACK CONVERSATION AREA. BUT WHICH CAME FIRST: THE ART OR ITS INSPIRATION?

MY BASEMENT STUDIO

An antique round farm table suggests fireside chats with friends. That friendly ambience is why Debbie selected it as the primary workstation for her basement studio. The chill of a hard-lined drafting table, she believes, would remove some warmth from her work—and it would alter the character of the room to that of a business. (And, when work is done, the table is perfect for coffee klatches or catching up on son Murphy's homework.)

Whether she's sketching new ideas for quilts or note cards, Debbie is armed with an eyeful of ammunition from this vantage point. Still lifes composed of beloved gifts and folk art, antique toys and animals, and, of course, her own quilts and other artwork, bring each corner of the room to one-of-a-kind life. But, she insists, you don't have to be an artist to live in an artful environment. Just group favorite objects together with an eye for balance, color, and texture.

MY BASEMENT STUDIO

Adding the mellow character of age into a new home is one thing for the main living spaces, but for the basement? Debbie's home is proof: Even here, it can be achieved. Start with antique furniture—nothing precious, just pieces that look long-lived, like this oak writing table and chair. Add vintage accessories, such as Debbie's old black rotary phone. Use paint to slather on years: This painted wall appears to be peeling plaster over bricks. If you're lucky enough to have windows in your basement, accentuate them as focal points. Debbie chose oak-stained wooden blinds to let in the light, then called attention to the window with shutters painted green. The final dressing is a window box overflowing with ivy and flowers. A recycled chair touched up in rainbow hues mirrors the blooming color.

Arranging accessories is child's play when you follow a few basic rules. Begin with your favorite objects. Group small pieces—such as the old metal garden forks shown here—for greater impact. Add foliage and flowers for color and texture.

BRING THE OUTDOORS IN WITH
EXTERIOR SHUTTERS AND A WINDOW BOX
TO BRIGHTEN ANY BASEMENT.

Debbie believes life is for the birds. They dominate her art and her artful home arrangements. An ivy-trailed trellis, set in an old screen door, is host to a ceramic bird, providing the perfect backdrop for her birdhouse-decorated cabinet.

Flea-market or curbside finds—or even unfinished new furniture—can become true treasures with nothing more than paint, brushes, and a little bit of whimsy. Debbie's friend reworked this bland cabinet into art by outlining each panel in black paint, which she wiped off for a distressed, aged look. Then, she painted the inside of each front panel white, for uniform backgrounds. After the paint dried, she gave each panel whimsical character by painting favorite Mumm motifs—a beehive, birdhouses, and bold, splashy sunflowers. Debbie encourages anyone to try their hand at artistry—but advises first sketching on paper, before drawing the design in pencil onto the furniture. Also, practice painting on an old scrap board. And don't worry if you think the results look amateurish or less than professional. A childlike quality has appeal all its own. If Debbie's encouragement still hasn't convinced you, try painting on patterns using stencils. They're a foolproof way to transform your old furniture into art.

Ensure focal-point status for your refinished furniture by topping it with compatible collections. Debbie's sampler provides a crowning finish to her carefree cats.

THE BIRD BATH

Attention to detail—down to the
black-and-ivory checkerboard border of
a tulip-laden tumbler—gives Debbie's
basement bathroom indelible charm.

What works in art, works in life. Debbie's bath captures the images she loves to depict in her art—old-looking painted wooden boards, picturesque gables, and a smattering of birds and flowers. The shower curtain and bath accessories are Debbie's design.

DEBBIE'S CHECKERBOARD PATTERN IN BLACK AND IVORY GIVES THE BATH ROLLICKING VISUAL RHYTHM.

Deciding on a design motif, then sticking to it, imbues any room with a cohesive quality. In Debbie's basement bathroom, the motif of choice is pediments—the same pitched rooflines that decorate her illustrations. Another design element—painted wood—is carried forth throughout the space. But the strongest statement is made when the pediments and painted woods unite.

The first painted-wood pediment appears in the big picture as a custom vanity mirror built onto the wall behind the sink. Suggesting the gable of a quaint cottage, the pediment's boards are individually painted a distressed rusty red and forest green, with portions stained a natural cedar hue. Just above the sink line, at the back-splash, the pediment is painted a cheery checkerboard black and ivory. Now for the details. The black-and-ivory border is repeated on towels, planters, a small table and bath mat, and even the shower curtain. The painted pediments also take a turn to miniature, appearing as folk-art birdhouses on the top shelf of a towel rack.

THE BIRD BATH

Even a bathroom fixture with as little inherent glamour as the stool can become a *pièce de résistance* with the right creative treatment. Debbie's solution: Nail up some weathered boards, paint for age, add a shingled A-frame roof—and the mundane stool becomes a clever indoor outhouse. Even a folk-art blackbird enjoys roosting here. But besides being creative, the stool surround is functional. Its two upper shelves provide storage for toiletries and decorative objects. The idea of an outhouse in the woods is further enhanced by a white picket fence—Debbie's re-invention of wainscoting—spanning the walls leading to the toilet. Even the toilet-paper holder fits the flight of fantasy, disguised as another wooden birdhouse.

ANY SPACE IN THE HOME—EVEN THE BASEMENT BATHROOM—CAN DISPLAY COTTAGE CHARM WHEN FRAMED IN A WHITE PICKET FENCE.

Debbie's whimsically designed hand towels become the cornerstones of a bathside vignette when topped with a folk art birdhouse and a bud vase of fresh blooms and ivy.

THE BIRD BATH

The angel bear hugging a doll in Debbie's upscale-country illustration gives her work lovable appeal. That same appeal is mirrored in the details of her home decor, which includes an angel bear in a flower basket on the basement-bath door.

Fool-the-eye trickery, which is what *trompe l'oeil* paintwork is all about, adds immediate interest to any room. When that room happens to be in the basement, the interest is magnified even more—for that space typically is relegated to bare-bones decorating. But Debbie's basement isn't typical. As her studio and favorite indoor retreat, it merits the same, if not more, design effort as any other area of her home. *Trompe l'oeil* painting not only dresses up one wall of the studio, it also adds instant age: The painted wall appears to be old plaster peeling over brick; the doors have all the charm of an old farmhouse. The result is a new home with a vintage feel.

But there's more to Debbie's basement than a vintage feel. There's another ingredient contributing to its warmth, which comes from careful accessorizing—attention to details. Warm, cuddly stuffed animals, such as the angel bear in a basket, provide visual hugs that adults, as well as kids, can appreciate.

VINTAGE VOGUE

An easy, peaceful feeling and glad
tidings characterize Debbie's art—and
her home. Both are touched with a
mood of whimsy.

VINTAGE VOGUE

S ophisticated comfort prevails in Debbie's living room. The comfort comes from generously proportioned overstuffed seating—feel-good pieces that invite curling up on. But even these fully upholstered pieces smack of a sophisticated eye. Fabrics include rich brocade and brushed velvet, teamed with more casual striped ticking. Dressmaker details such as contrasting welting and fringe skirting add a fine finish, and plump pillows complete the cozy setting.

The palette is garden fresh. Pastels—especially pinks—mix with pale, faded greens for a look that's vintage vogue. Even accessories such as the Degas ballerina feature the pinks of summer flowers.

VINTAGE VOGUE

The uncontested focal point of the living room is the hearth. With the mantel shelf and molding outlined in shimmering gold, the fireplace has a faux-marble finish in deep green, mottled with gold, to suggest depth and texture. (Look for the same faux-marble finish in Debbie's dining room, in the next chapter.) Both the green and the gold are repeated throughout the living room, often subtlely, on accessories. Vintage books, brass candlesticks, a wall mirror, and other objects have golden sparkle. Even a papier-mâché urn is hand-painted gold and green. Other accessories, such as a painted lamp, lighten the mood with pastels.

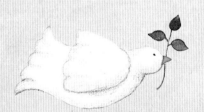

SOPHISTICATION AND COMFORT CAN BE COMPATIBLE. RICH GREENS AND GOLDS, LIGHTENED WITH CHEERY PASTELS, ENSURE A MOOD THAT'S ELEGANT BUT NEVER INTIMIDATING.

DINING ROOM

A genteel spirit abides in Debbie's
dining room, where guests are nurtured
with a visual feast that's as beautifully
composed as any work of art.

DINING ROOM

alancing elegance and livability in home design can be a daunting challenge, but Debbie rises to the task with ease. No space illustrates this more than her dining room. A tabletop laden with cut glass and crystal, as well as white lace and a spring bouquet centerpiece, declares a formal mood. But not for long. Balancing the elegance are more casual elements. The furnishings themselves—an antique oak table and Windsor chairs—feature a farmhouse flavor with their turned legs and humble finish. The message is clear: Dining is a civilized affair, but one to be enjoyed. Even dressed at its best, this room feels like home.

The spring-fresh garden ambience that wends its way throughout the home also lends a hand in making the dining room eminently livable. A ficus tree draws up close to a window. At its feet rests a sampling of potted plants. The window treatment underscores the garden feel. White blinds ensure privacy, while a dropped rod draped in white sheers entwined with ivy suggests breezy springtime pleasures all year long.

DINING ROOM

An antique china cabinet continues the farmhouse flavor of the oak table and chairs. But there's nothing quaint about this room. Sophistication is clearly at work, especially around the edges. The wainscoting that wraps the lower walls features the same elegant mottled green faux-marble finish with gold molding highlights seen on the living room's fireplace.

Another element contributing to the space's upscale design is its incorporation of the unexpected. The best-designed rooms unfold surprises. In this case, the unexpected takes the form of a dress-maker's dummy painted in military attire. Tucked in a corner, the oddball piece commands attention—and recognition of Debbie's skill at introducing eccentricity. Illuminating the dining experience is an earthy vintage chandelier.

Spring bouquets aren't just for vases. These freshly cut blooms can't be overlooked in their unlikely vessels—a gathering of five glass bottles in an old metal carrier. Searching your kitchen cupboards may produce worthy "vases" you never considered.

DINING ROOM

Entertaining is one of Debbie's delights. It's evident in her playful coffee cup illustrations, and in the coffee spread she presents to guests.

The small size of Debbie's dining room proves no obstacle for entertaining in style. What the dining table can't accommodate, other furnishings can. Every square inch of existing furniture is enlisted into service. Even this small, two-drawer painted table becomes a receptacle for a showy display of china cups and saucers and dessert plates—it can serve as a mini sideboard, or a non-portable dessert cart.

But there is one catch in accommodating the overflow: Pay attention to details. Any table used for serving must be dressed for the occasion. Debbie includes mismatched cut-glass vases with fresh flowers to decorate this small table—accessories scaled to fit the table's diminutive size, yet ever-festive. Resting on a real lace doily, even the silver truffle dish is decorated with a fresh-flower sprig.

FAMILY ROOM

Star-spangled, snow-kissed images of
Christmas shower Debbie's seasonal
designs—and her own home's cozy
den—with warmth and joy.

FAMILY ROOM

A big brick fireplace, built-in wooden bookshelves, and plump sink-down furnishings upholstered in Beacon-blanket fabrics make Debbie's den an idyllic backdrop for Christmas decorations. Her approach to the holidays takes the warm side of traditional, with an Americana accent rooted deep in country style. Colors are traditional deep reds and forest greens. Her fabric panels on pillows sprinkle hearty ho-ho-hos across chair backs and the floor. Baskets of fresh-cut evergreens join robust poinsettias to splash the holiday palette into every nook and corner. A cut tree is laden with handmade and cast ornaments Debbie designed, and a forest of wooden folk-art trees shades the mantel. At the light of a match, the hearth blazes holiday radiance throughout the room.

A small, berry-spangled wreath inset with a primitive country-style star is the focal point for a mantel vignette that includes garlands of greenery and fresh fruit for color.

FAMILY ROOM

Functioning like a greatroom, with a casual dining area as well as a living space, the den is perfect for informal holiday entertaining. Guests can appreciate the table, festively decorated in seasonal attire, without ever having to leave the warmth of the fire or the sparkle of twinkle lights on the Christmas tree. But even at its most informal, Debbie's table always expresses personal style. Most of the tabletop pieces, from coffee mugs to napkins, are her own designs. A basket of country-red apples accented with just a sprig of holiday greens joins a pair of folk-art Santas for a no-fuss centerpiece. Favorite holiday cards stand as art.

Debbie's holiday dinnerware includes snowman mugs and coordinated plates. Even plain checked napkins gain a wintry attitude when tied with a single snowman ornament.

WHETHER IT'S FRESH GINGERBREAD MEN OR PIPING-HOT CIDER, CHRISTMAS APPEALS TO THE SENSES.

Keep The Christmas Spirit All Year Long

FAMILY ROOM

With its ready-made warmth that lasts all year long, Debbie's den is a natural recipient for her artful holiday accents. Framed and matted crafts projects that might be a little too primitive for her more formal rooms snuggle in, right at home, on the den walls. And that's a holiday decorating approach Debbie recommends for others, too. Not every room of the house must be decorated for Christmas in exactly the same fashion. Choose your friendliest, most feel-good public space for holiday treatments that are whimsical, fun, and folksy. Then, unify all the rooms with more subtle threads of seasonal continuity, such as cut greens that are swagged, draped, or injected in accessories as holiday accents.

The simple lines and childlike form of Debbie's holiday snowman appeals to the child in all of us. Her snowmen are available now on a wide range of home accessories, fabrics, and cross-stitch patterns.

LET THE GOOD NEWS OF CHRISTMAS
RING FROM THE ROOFTOPS.

Whimsical Ornaments

are symbols of the seasons' good cheer! Debbie loves to decorate her home with a fantasy collection of adorable ornaments that celebrate winter, Christmas, even gardening.

Paper Portraits

are picture-perfect gifts for everyone on your holiday list. The sturdy die-cut cardboard frames become three-dimensional backdrops for classic Debbie Mumm motifs—an angel, hearts, and friendly felines.

HOLIDAY INSPIRATIONS

Whatever the season, whatever the
occasion, you can tell friends and family
how much they mean to you with a gift
item featuring one of Debbie's designs.

Paper Capers start with simple shapes and colorful textured paper. Use these holiday brights for special ornaments to trim the tree or a package.

Holiday Frame-ups

feature some of Debbie's most beloved seasonal images. Beautiful matted color prints become merry masterpieces when displayed in handsome wood frames enhanced with Debbie's signature borders.

Santa Scenes

adorn the collectible porcelain
plates produced by Franklin
Mint. They hold a special
place in Debbie's home and
are sure to become highly
prized decorating accents for
your holiday home.

Artful Buttons on a Nine-

patch block are just a sampling of the fun
you can have mixing and matching Debbie's
fanciful folk art images. With dozens of
ceramic buttons such as the ones shown
here, it only takes minutes to make
masterpieces in miniature!

The Magic of Santa

comes to life on fabric panels to deck the home with holiday spirit. Debbie's signature-style Santas steal the show on everything from plump pillows to plates, to centerpiece placemats!

Three Jolly Snowmen

add a triple measure of cheer to Debbie's holiday decor. Soft-sculptured from cotton and snuggled in knitted caps and scarves, this charming trio is sure to bring smiles and a warm welcome to chilly friends and family.

Christmas Toys and Joys are just a snippet away! Holly Designs (562-946-4167), transforms scraps of favorite Debbie Mumm fabrics into quick upholstery for their small-scale wooden furniture. You can purchase this inviting collection for a special doll or nestle it into a vintage-vogue mantel or tabletop display of your creation.

HALLOWEEN

When the moon is full and the bat's on wing—at least in home decorating accents, you'll know it's Halloween. Debbie prepares for this children's holiday with traditional motifs given her unique, folksy spin. Harvest pumpkins line the perimeters of her designs. And pumpkins carved as jack-o-lanterns wend their way into other crafts projects. With backs arched, black cats create visual rhythm through repetition, in other designs. The palette is strictly orange and black—but rendered in her signature checkerboard pattern. The whole house doesn't have to spell Halloween—just an accent, strategically placed here and there, is enough to delight both children and adults.

AUTUMN SIGNALS HARVEST TIME
AND HALLOWEEN, BOTH REFLECTED IN
DEBBIE'S OFFERINGS.

White crescent moons, gold stars, and orange spinning orbs splattered across a black-sky background, which is bordered in black-and-ivory checks, provides a more subtle suggestion of Halloween's mysterious mood.

PEACE & QUIET

Sweet dreams, Debbie-style, are
watched over by angels in a room that's so
restful it could soothe any weary soul.

PEACE & QUIET

As the most personal space in the home, the bedroom mirrors the personality—especially the personal preferences—of those who live in it. It's no surprise to those familiar with Debbie's reputation as a quilter that her bed is layered in fine quilts and coverlets. Her characteristic earth tones—deep, rich reds, muted greens, and soft browns—decorate the quilts and establish the palette of the room. What may come as a surprise, however, is the room's turn toward antiquity—not 19th-century country-farmhouse style, but that of classical Greece and Rome. Thanks to the proportions of columns flanking the bed, the entire room acquires an air of grandeur.

The pediment theme found in other rooms of Debbie's home reappears in the bedroom, but this time in its simplest form. A plain pediment of molding crowns the wall above the bed, suggesting the ancient architecture of the Parthenon. Mounted just beneath it, a golden cherub softens the hard lines. Symmetrical placement of art and candlestick lamps creates formal balance. Artful paintwork fools the eye with unexpected scenes at the windows and doors.

Fine craftsmanship and personal inscriptions reveal Debbie's popularity with the friends and staff who made this quilt for her. The muted earth-tone palette of her quilts establishes the color scheme of the entire room, which includes ample ivory backgrounds for serenity.

PEACE & QUIET

Judging by its appearance in her artwork, checkerboard tops the list of Debbie's favorite geometric pattern motifs. In her bedroom, which is a testament to her favorite things, checkerboard patterns appear again, but in subtle form. Instead of the bold, splashy black-and-ivory checks taking center stage, they're restricted to a pencil-thin border of welting on the upholstered furniture in a sitting area. A second border of red welting teams up with the black and ivory to maximize interest. Green and black checks also decorate the main upholstery fabric—but the colors are so dark as to appear almost neutral and solid from a distance.

More than just a place to sleep for the night, Debbie's master bedroom contains the stuff of sweet daydreams, too. A pair of comfortable rolled-arm chairs are perfect for reading or taking tea or coffee. A matching ottoman doubles as a serving table.

BEDROOMS ARE FOR THE NURTURING OF BODY AND SPIRIT—AND A LITTLE FINERY GETS THE JOB OFF TO A JUMP START.

Peace & Quiet

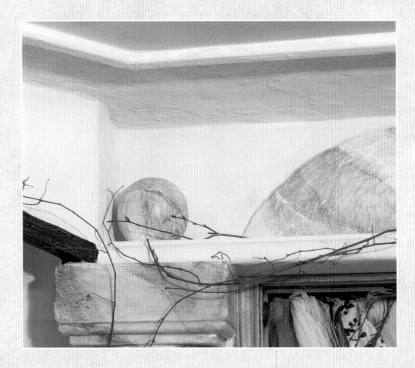

The cypresses of Tuscany dot distant hills 'seen' through a pair of French doors opening onto Debbie's master bathroom. No, her home is not a Tuscan villa but a new home in Spokane, Washington. The hills and trees are part of a *trompe l'oeil* mural painted on the door lights, enhancing the room's ambience of antiquity. A pair of columns flanking the doors have a faux-marble finish, suggesting the same rich mood and classical period. On the wall above, the paintwork takes its cues from nature, going sky blue with spongy, white clouds.

The decorative paint treatments are Debbie's solution to obtaining the fantasy bedroom of her dreams. Close inspection of every wall reveals an artist's handiwork. In some areas, the paint is daubed on thick, for the look of aging plaster. Debbie also draped twig branches across moldings, columns, and windows to suggest an indoor garden of old. The message the room reveals regarding its occupant is clear: Her thoughts are sky high, and heaven-bound.

MURPHY'S ROOM

A young boy's bedroom is a parent's
opportunity to design a future. For
Debbie's son, Murphy, the future looks
full of love and creativity.

MURPHY'S ROOM

Designing a growing boy's bedroom means putting aside your own fondness for cutesy, cuddly kid themes that would soon be age-inappropriate and stagnate development. What's needed are design elements that reflect who the boy is now—and that nurture who he may become. In short, what's needed is room to grow.

Murphy's room provides just that. Debbie's favorite quilt palette of earth tones will last Murphy through adulthood. But their appearance as large color blocks, with a different hue painted on each wall, offers enough stimulation to appeal to a child. Instead of babyish shelving or too-grown-up chests, modular stacking blocks provide flexibility for all stages and ages. The blocks can be rearranged as needs change, along with the objects displayed. This open storage tidies up the room, while leaving plenty of eye appeal to keep a young mind motivated. Even the desk knows no age restrictions. For now, it's a play area—but it's computer-ready for later.

MURPHY'S ROOM

Murphy's room is proof: Decorative and functional elements need not be at odds. Debbie combines both to meet Murphy's lifestyle needs while ensuring that his aesthetic sensibilities also get plenty of visual strokes. Every child has a need for—plus, simply enjoys—a bulletin board. It's a place to tack up the latest relay ribbons, school papers, art, or trading cards. And, it's also a good training ground for encouraging responsibility: A child's own "to-do" list can be prominently posted as a positive reminder (more positive than a parent's nagging). But instead of the plain-vanilla version, Debbie's choice of bulletin board is a continuation of the color-blocks design she used for the walls—and in none other than her signature checkerboard pattern. Cork tiles painted varying hues line one section of wall, repeating the room's palette.

MURPHY'S ROOM

Murphy's room pays homage to a boy's best friend. Debbie's tribute to dogs, as artwork or framing a friend's favorite pooch, appears on tabletops and the walls. Checkerboard borders leave no doubt as to the artist's identity.

Just as a grown-up's bedroom is a private retreat, so is a child's. It's a place to be surrounded by reminders of passions and pleasures—from sports to beloved pets. Murphy's love of baseball is creatively reflected in a nondescript furniture piece Debbie customized for one-of-a-kind character. Collage-style, she covered the furnishing with baseball cards. Paying the same attention to detail as elsewhere in the home, she even created a unique drawer pull out of an actual baseball—a clever twist on the idea of hardware knobs. A closet door becomes both storage and display when dotted with mounts for baseball caps. A bat, ball and glove, and sneakers feel right at home.

A ROOM THAT'S DECORATED IN FAVORITE THINGS HELPS A CHILD FEEL SAFE, SECURE, AND ABUNDANTLY HAPPY.

MURPHY'S BATH

A nautical theme, full of whimsical
delight, creates a child-worthy splash in
the bath. Who would have thought
bathtime could be such fun?

fortune spent on high-end fixtures and deluxe building materials isn't necessary to design a child's bath that smacks of style. Starting with a simple vanity topped in ocean-blue tile and outfitted with a standard sink, Debbie gave her son's bathroom a high-seas character. She introduced the nautical theme with the painted wall and her coordinated shower curtain, both depicting a regatta of sailboats gently rolling across

foamy blue waves. The motif is repeated on another of Debbie's designs, this time a print matted in her cheery yellow-and-blue check fabric and mounted in a blue frame. The pattern also appears in the sailboat design itself, as skinny borders that undulate as below-the-surface waves. Other accessories—starfish, buoy, jar of seashells, toy wooden sailboat, and tin pail painted with suns and sailboats (which has the functional dual purpose of caddying wash cloths)—underscore the theme. The serpentine form of Debbie's to-and-fro sea sets the entire room reeling in the rockabye rhythms of waves.

Murphy's Bath

When the person accessorizing the bath happens to be a designer like Debbie, open storage often is the best bet. Instead of hiding functional items such as bath towels and toiletries behind closed (and costly) cabinet doors, she reasons, why not arrange them artfully, so that they're decorative, too? The textures of a wooden handled woven basket add warmth to the bath's cooler ceramic surfaces. But instead of being a space guzzler, with for-looks-only function, the basket is enlisted by Debbie as a hand-towel holder. Then, plopping the basket directly onto the floor, she integrates it into the room by adding other accessories to create a picture-perfect still life. A school of starfish nuzzle up close, along with a blue buoy and a Mason jar full of beachcombing finds.

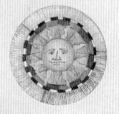

ANY SPACE BECOMES AN ARTIST'S CANVAS
WHEN TREATED WITH INTERESTING OBJECTS
THAT PAUSE THE EYE.

Home Away From Home

Like the sunflowers that decorate Debbie's desk, her design business Mumm's The Word is flourishing. From its roots in country-quilt patterns, it has branched into home-decor, gift, and stationery products.

HOME AWAY FROM HOME

In 1986, on a leap of faith, Debbie Mumm bought a plane ticket to Houston to display her quilt patterns at a booth she'd rented at the International Quilt Market trade show held there. She was nervous about the investment. She charged plane fare and booth, plus hotel, on her credit card—hoping to write enough orders to pay off the bill.

No problem. The credit card debt was paid off immediately with a nonstop string of orders. This giant leap of faith not only landed Debbie squarely on her feet, but it gave her new business, Mumm's The Word, a fast-running start to international acclaim.

Now, thanks to continued burgeoning growth, the business has expanded into a new, custom-built, million-dollar facility that spans 10,000 square feet. Having long outgrown her basement studio, as well as two away-from-home locations that followed it, Debbie needed the new space to accommodate her ever-growing art department and studio, sewing room, desktop publishing department, offices and warehouse, and sales and shipping headquarters.

To meet the evergrowing need for new designs and products, in May
of 1997, Mumm's The Word moved into a 10,000-square-foot building
constructed on a one-acre site in Spokane, Washington. Marking a
decade of progress, the new headquarters is in sharp contrast to the
quaint Craftsman-style bungalow where, in 1986, Debbie began
designing patterns in the dining room.

HOME AWAY FROM HOME

The business that began with quilting patterns and easy-to-make crafts projects has diversified into a full-service design business that has penetrated all areas of home decor, accessories, gift items, and stationery. But despite the phenomenal growth, Mumm's The Word still has a friendly flavor.

With the ongoing and growing demand for her books, patterns, and fabrics, Debbie continues to sketch and paint, while Steve Mumm actively pursues licensing of the designs. In less than three years, their united efforts have resulted in more than 80 licensed products, featuring Debbie Mumm designs on everything from fabric to note cards to coffee mugs.

"DEBBIE IS INCREDIBLY IN TUNE TO TRENDS, BOTH GIFTS AND HOME INTERIORS." —STEVE MUMM

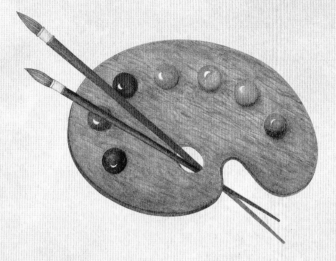

WORK BOOK

Inspired by all you've seen and read? Then get out the drop cloths and paintbrushes because on the following pages Debbie and her friends tell you how they transformed Debbie's house into her dream home! Debbie even asked the friendly folks at Plaid, the crafts-paint and paint-accessory people, for step-by-step instructions for some of the painting techniques that were used.
So now you, too, can employ some of the techniques to personalize your home.

Debbie Mumm I began designing quilt patterns in 1986, in the dining room of the Craftsman-style bungalow we lived in at the time. The business grew too large for the house and required its own quarters. I moved into a new home as well and had a great time decorating and embellishing it...with the help of some very talented friends!

I am often asked if I will ever run out of ideas. My response is negative! I live and breathe what I do. This is my world. There are always millions of ideas for inspiration. Better yet, I've always believed that if I can do it—you can, too!

Jackie Saling For ten years I taught painting classes in a store that specialized in decorative painting and wall treatments.

The business closed, and I applied at Mumm's The Word for an Art Studio Assistant position and got the job! I paint, help with fabric layout and design, and do pretty much any job that needs to be done. My favorite part of the work is the painting. I do a lot of furniture, wall, and display painting for photo shoots and shows. My motto is "If it sits still, it can be painted."

I love working for Debbie. She's a unique, creative person and allows me the freedom to use my talents in many ways. Laughter is a big part of our day as we work together to meet many deadlines. Some days it's hard to believe they call this work!

Lynn Guier I've been an artist all my life. I had just completed a restoration of an old brewery, turning it into shops and restaurants with Bill Mound, when I met Debbie Mumm in Spokane. My teaming up with Bill proved to be the perfect match in creating the work Debbie had us do.

Debbie is a very warm-hearted woman who is a joy to work with, even under stressful conditions. I think her art work illustrates what Debbie is like at heart. She is extremely creative and at the same time down to earth and knows how to get things done. She understands synergy—how to create with others. I found myself joyfully challenged to create something that would really delight her. She allowed me to do what I do best. Debbie, Bill, and I were very pleased with the outcome.

WORK BOOK

Stephanie Puddy I am a native of Spokane, where I went to school for graphic design. I moved to Los Angeles in 1983 and began freelancing as a photostylist, as well as painting backdrops and surfaces.

Three years ago I moved back to the Pacific Northwest, where I find the environment more appealing. I now do faux finishes, custom painting, murals, surfaces, backdrops, and photostyling as well.

I met Debbie through a local photographer. Debbie's home is an environment of beautiful furnishings. Many have an eclectic elegance that lends itself to gold-leafing, marbleizing, and washes.

I enjoyed working with Debbie, who openly volunteered her home as a creative palette for the imagination of myself and many other artists.

Nancy Eubanks I've lived in Spokane for 18 years. I am a stay-at-home mom with three children. My hobbies have always been painting, gardening, and collecting 'old junk.'

I love finding stuff in second-hand stores or yard sales, then painting them and turning them into treasures. Many of my creations are for sale at a local gift shop. In fact, Debbie and I met at this gift shop and we've done business together ever since.

Meet Debbie and her artistic friends. These women with talent, vision, and good taste, have made miracles in a plain, white-walled builder's home. Using surface-decorating techniques such as marbleizing and faux wood-graining, they've put a personal stamp on nearly every available surface. Read their project descriptions, then do-it-yourself with the easy instructions listed below!

MY BASEMENT STUDIO
& BIRD BATH

- TELEVISION CABINET ● FAUX BRICK WALLS

- WALLS ● FLOOR CLOTH ● OUTHOUSE FACADE

TELEVISION CABINET
By Nancy Eubanks

Page 21 I used Debbie's designs for my color palette. I applied the base colors, then sanded the edges. An antiquing-gel finish provided a worn, aged look. Using Debbie's drawings, I sketched and then painted the pictures.

FAUX BRICK WALLS
By Nancy Eubanks

Pages 18, 29 I sketched areas on the walls where I wanted the brick to come through. I lightly brushed on the bricks with a terra-cotta color, randomly adding darker shades to avoid uniformity. Gray was brushed in the cracks and I highlighted the brick edges with dark brown.

WORK BOOK

WALLS
By Stephanie Puddy
Page 14 For a watercolor look, I used hydra sponges to apply a multicolor wash of latex paints which I thinned with faux-finishing glaze.

FLOORCLOTH
By Jackie Saling
Page 25 I used a primed canvas purchased in a crafts store for the floorcloth. The design was painted with acrylic crafts paint.

When the painting was complete, I folded under the cloth's edges about 1 inch, applied tacky glue in the fold, and clamped the edges with clothes pins for a finished edge. I varnished the painted surface with three to four coats of a non-yellowing acrylic crafts varnish.

OUTHOUSE FACADE
By Lynn Guier
Page 26 SUPPLIES
- Cedar boards
- Cedar shingles for roof
- White-pine boards
- Outdoor lantern
- Paint: red and green
- Gel stain: raw umber
- Sandpaper
- Nails and glue
- Wooden dowel
- Skill- and bandsaw, knife

PREPARATION

I sandblasted and edge-carved the cedar boards for the sides, back, and face pieces. After cutting the pieces to size, I used a bandsaw to cut a crescent moon in the center top of the cedar board.

I painted the top faceplates red and the side faceplates green, then wiped them both with stain. A hole was drilled into the top of the red faceplate to accomodate the lamp wiring.

Using a bandsaw, I cut a blackbird body and wing from white pine; I carved and sanded the edges, and drilled two holes in the bottom of the bird's body for dowel legs.

The shelves are white pine that I carved, sanded, and wiped with stain.

INSTALLATION

Nail the boards to the back and side walls. Place the shelves atop the horizontal cedar boards nailed to the side walls. Nail the green faceplates to the sides.

Attach the red A-frame faceplates. Glue roof planks atop the red A-frame faceplate and the back-wall cedar boards. Glue shingles to the roof planks.

Attach the lamp and run the wires. Drill two holes in the roof and insert the bird's dowel legs.

My Basement Studio & Bird Bath

Sink and Vanity
By Lynn Guier
Page 25 SUPPLIES

- Slate pieces with interesting shapes
- Beaten-brass round bar sink
- Faucet
- Grout
- Colored grout
- Cedar boards
- ¼" plywood for painted door panels
- ¾" plywood for basic vanity base and top
- ¼" Wonder board
- Screws; wood glue
- Carved and sandblasted cedar for door frames
- Fine chicken wire
- Paint: red, green, black, and raw umber
- Gel stain: raw umber
- Dark green spray paint
- Prisma colored pencils

PREPARATION

To add space and interest to the small room, we removed the existing vanity and placed the new one at an angle.

INSTALLATION

We arranged slate in an interesting design, keeping in mind the size and placement of the sink. The outer edges of the design were kept irregular.

We cut Wonder board and a ¾" plywood top to fit the slate design, we then cut a hole to accomodate the sink.

After painting the ¼" plywood with background color, we used colored pencils to draw the birdhouses and other items. The pencils create a diffused effect.

THE MIRROR was made with a plywood back, in which we cut a curved opening for the mirror. Cedar planks make up the back, and white pine boards with carved edges are painted green for the shutters.

OUTDOOR LANTERNS were wired in place of the old light fixture. We used the same colors used elsewhere in the room. All painted surfaces were antiqued with a raw umber gel stain. A planter box with Debbie's logo checkerboard design sits atop the counter and is attached to the entire structure.

Wall Cupboards
By Lynn Guier
Page 25 SUPPLIES

- Cedar boards
- Hook and eye latches
- Fine chicken wire
- ¼" plywood
- Hinges
- Paint: green, black, and raw umber
- Colored pencils

PREPARATION

We removed the doors and frame from the original linen closet.

For the new doors, I sandblasted, carved, and painted back panels green. I painted ¼" plywood panels with black and raw umber, then used colored pencils to draw a shelf and items you'd find in a potting shed.

INSTALLATION

To complete the door panels, I spray-painted chicken wire and sandwiched it between the panel and a cedar frame. I installed the doors with hinges and completed the rustic look by using hook-and-eye latches.

CEILING AND WALLS
By Lynn Guier

I applied touches of pale blue and gold paint to the white ceiling and walls, to create a very subtle sky with clouds.

TOWEL RACK
By Lynn Guier
Page 24 SUPPLIES

- White-pine boards
- Cedar boards
- Cedar stick
- Paint: red, yellow, green, and black
- Gel stain: raw umber
- L brackets
- Drill, jigsaw

PREPARATION

For the post, I sandblasted and carved a cedar board. I cut cedar for the top plate and used white pine for the bottom. The birdhouses are white pine, which painted and stained. I used a drill and jigsaw to make holes in the birdhouses.

INSTALLATION

I first nailed the cedar post to the wall, then put together the cedar and pine plates. I attached the birdhouses to the horizontal plate from underneath, mounted the L brackets to the backs of the birdhouses, and attached them to the wall.

I then used screws to secure a stick horizontally onto the upright cedar for towels.

VINTAGE VOGUE

- FIREPLACE

- WALLS

- LAMP

FIREPLACE
By Stephanie Puddy
Page 34 CROWN MOLDING
I gold-leafed the molding, then applied a dark green wash over it and wiped it down for an interesting antique look.

SURROUND
The surround was originally shiny brass. I sanded it and sprayed it with metal primer, then used a patina kit sold in craft stores.

TRIM
I painted the trim with liquid gold leaf, then followed with a dark green wash to antique it.

MARBLEIZED MANTEL

SUPPLIES

- Sea sponges, feathers, fine-tipped brushes
- Paint: artist's acrylics and latex paint mixed with faux-finishing glaze. Oil-based paints may be used as well.
- Clear semi-gloss acrylic spray

I used variations of forest greens, mixing these with black and white, and some browns, to make grey greens, very dark greens, lighter greens, etc. These variations add depth. I primed the bare wood and applied a white base coat, then randomly sponged the area with the greens, allowing white to show through in areas. I built layers of these various colors, adding veins between coats until I had achieved the sense of marble. I accented the veins to complete the various areas, and then

applied several coats of clear semi-gloss acrylic spray to protect and seal.

WALLS
By Stephanie Puddy

Page 34 Using hydra sponges, I applied a multicolored wash of latex paints, thinned with faux-finishing glaze for a watercolor look.

LAMP
By Nancy Eubanks

Page 34 The fabric fringe and lampshade were purchased at a fabric store. I covered the sticky lampshade base with fabric, then glued fringe around the lower edge. I painted an old base to coordinate with the fabric. Then I sanded and antiqued it to give it an old look.

CHAIR RAIL AND WINDOW TRIM
By Stephanie Puddy
Page 40 I painted the chair rail and window trim with liquid gold leaf, then followed with a dark green wash for an antique effect.

UPPER WALLS
By Stephanie Puddy
Page 40 For the upper walls, I used hydra sponges to apply a multicolored wash of latex paints, thinned with faux-finishing glaze for a watercolor look.

DINING ROOM

- CHAIR RAIL AND WINDOW TRIM

- MARBLEIZED LOWER WALLS

- CURTAIN ROD

WORK BOOK

MARBLEIZED LOWER WALLS
By Stephanie Puddy

Page 40 For tools, I used natural sponges, feathers, and fine-tipped brushes.

I used artist's acrylics and latex paints, mixed with glaze, in variations of forest green, black, white, and brown, then mixed them to make grey greens, very dark greens, lighter greens, etc. The color variations add depth.

I then randomly sponged the area with the greens, allowing the original white wall to show through in some spots. I continued to build layers of these various colors, adding veins in between coats until I achieved a sense of marble. I then accented the veins to complete the various areas.

Lastly, several coats of clear semi-gloss acrylic spray were applied to protect and seal.

CURTAIN ROD
By Stephanie Puddy

Page 40 I spray-painted the rod with a matte brown color. When dry, I randomly sponged on off-white and gold paints.

WALLS
By Lynn Guier

Page 62 The walls in Debbie's bedroom were covered in the mud mixture (see page 103, Preparation—Arch, third paragraph). The walls have a subtle texture that is done by applying small lumps of mud with a trowel, then brushing it down with a soft brush and clean water.

I painted the walls a pale honey color, then washed with a darker honey color. The wash was the darker color mixed with Flotrol and applied to the wall with cheese cloth.

PEACE & QUIET

- WALLS   ● SHELVING   ● ARCH & COLUMNS

- MOLDING   ● PAINTED DOOR & WINDOW PANELS

WORK BOOK

WRAPAROUND SHELVING
By Lynn Guier

Page 66 The shelving that runs around the room is made from plywood and has a lip on the outside edge to hide the lighting track that runs along the wall.

The lighting track allows any number of small lights to be plugged in anywhere an accent is needed on the shelf. The light is controlled by a dimmer switch with a remote control.

The shelving was coated with the mud mixture. The marble-looking balls are Styrofoam balls that were covered with drywall mud, then sanded, painted, and color-penciled to match the faux columns. The colors of the pencils range from sepia, terra cotta, warm grey, and medium grey, to white.

MOLDING, ETC.
By Lynn Guier

Page 62 All the molding around the doors and floor was painted with gold, then crackle, then the raw umber/black mix, then clear coated. I even had the carpet dyed a custom color.

The dresser next to the bed and the entertainment piece were designed specifically to match existing pieces.

PAINTED PANELS
By Lynn Guier

Pages 62, 67 I painted the outer edges of the doors dark with cracked effects and made an inner panel of ⅛" plywood framed with molding and actual muntins. I painted the panel to resemble a Mediterranean countryside. We attached the panels to the doors. I made the *trompe l'oeil* window in the same way.

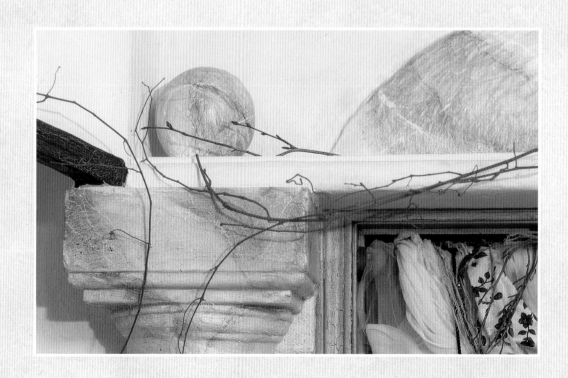

PEACE & QUIET

ARCH AND COLUMNS
By Lynn Guier
Page 67 SUPPLIES—ARCH

- Pine strips and ¼" plywood for boxed arch
- Carpet board (¾" thick, hard fiberboard)
- Floor and adhesive (glue)
- 3" old paintbrush
- Cast-plaster girl's face
- Utility knife

SUPPLIES—COLUMNS

- Cardboard construction tubes (two sizes)
- Garden hose
- ¼" tubing
- Plywood
- Drywall mud
- Sand
- White glue

WORK BOOK

PREPARATION—ARCH

To make an arch and colums such as Debbie's, first construct an arch box with a white pine frame. Cover the frame with a ¼" plywood skin.

Using a tablesaw, cut carpet board into brick sizes, then carve the edges with a utility knife. Glue the bricks onto the plywood.

Mix one box of drywall premix with two cups of sand and two cups of white glue. Brush the mud mixture into the spaces between the bricks and all over the bricks. Let the mixture set for 15–30 minutes, depending on humidity, and then, with a clean brush and clean water, smooth it over the entire area.

PREPARATION—COLUMNS

Prepare the mud mixture. For use on the columns, it is best if the mud is mixed the day before and covered.

Using a bandsaw, cut round tops and bases for columns out of stacked plywood, cutting them the same circumference as the larger tube. Strip the tubes of any wax coating and fill the grooves. Cut slices off the larger tube and place a slice between two plywood rounds for a column base; repeat for a top.

Toe-nail three 12" pieces of 2x4 to the center of the base's top round. Place the narrower tube on the base; screw the tube to the 2x4s; repeat for the top.

The smaller decorative bands are made from garden hose, thin tubing, and rope that is nailed and glued around the columns.

INSTALLATION

Debbie's columns wrap around a corner, so we cut away ¼ of the columns. We screwed wood strips to the wall, then attached the columns to the strips.

We placed the arch atop the columns, let the mud set, smoothed it out with water, let it dry, and filled any cracks with Spackle.

We base-coated the columns to match the walls, followed by a wash of several warm honey-brown colors and an additional darker tone.

Details such as cracks were done with colored pencils. Finally, we applied crystal clear varnish to the colums.

WALLS AND CEILING
By Lynn Guier

Murphy was allowed to pick the theme for his room, then Debbie set to work with her designs. I designed around her projects.

Page 70 The walls and ceiling were all painted in different colors. The effect was done by painting a pastel color with a wash of a purer color on top. This captured the feel and color of Debbie's fabrics. The carpet was dyed for a custom match.

The storage boxes were made individually and each side was painted a different color to match the walls. They can be turned or stacked in many different ways.

MURPHY'S ROOM & BATH

- WALLS & CEILING
- BASEBALL-CARD BED STAND
- MEASURING TAPE
- SAILBOAT PAIL
- STENCILED WALL

MEASURING TAPE
By Lynn Guier

Page 72 The wide molding separating the two rooms that comprise Murphy's space needed something, and my carpenter's tape inspired this actual foot-by-foot measurement.

I painted using the same technique I used on the walls: a lighter color with a pure color sponged on top. I determined the size and style for the numbers and ordered them from my local art-supply store; they are vinyl cut-outs. The lines are vinyl tape.

I kid-proofed it with four coats of a clear finish.

BASEBALL-CARD BED STAND
By Lynn Guier

Page 75 SUPPLIES
- Packs of baseball cards
- Decoupage medium; glue
- Five baseballs
- Utility knife; scissors
- Drill, ½" bit
- Dowels

CREATING

To make a bed stand such as the one in Murphy' room, drill dowel holes in the five baseballs, in the drawer, and in the base.

Position cards in overlapping patterns that balance color and design, turning the figures to avoid a definite direction. One at a time, glue the cards to the top of the stand, allowing them to fold over the edge. Cut excess at the bottom with a utility knife.

Apply enough layers of decoupage medium to the card-covered areas to smooth out the overlapping card edges.

Cut and glue the dowels into the baseballs and insert into the drawer and bottom holes.

PAINTED WALL
By Jackie Saling

Page 79 I basecoated the wall with a light value of color and then sponged with two darker values of the same color. I used sea sponges—one for each color works best. The sponging mixture consists of 1 part waterbase varnish, 2 parts water and 1 part acrylic craft paint. This mixture makes a very durable, washable wall surface.

I traced a sailboat design onto the wall with graphite paper. Then I painted it to coordinate with the fabric shower curtain.

SAILBOAT PAIL
By Jackie Saling

Page 79 If the tin pail is new, wash it with vinegar and dry well. If the pail is old, first remove any rust before painting.

Paint the pail with flat spray primer. Paint or stencil a design with acrylic craft paint. Finish with two coats of spray varnish.

HOME AWAY FROM HOME

- DRAFTING TABLE
- DISPLAY CABINET
- RECYCLING CAN
- FRAMES

DRAFTING TABLE
By Jackie Saling

Page 82 This was an antique table that we wanted to paint decoratively. The areas that were to be repainted were first sanded well to dull the surface.

The red background was painted over a crackle finish that had been applied over a black background. The checkerboard and sunflowers were painted and then a surface crackle finish was applied over the painted area. This type of crackle is smaller and more subtle than the large background crackle.

Once dry, I sanded the painted areas to create a distressed look. Then an antiquing medium was applied.

I finished it with a matte spray varnish.

WORK BOOK

DISPLAY CABINET
By Jackie Saling

Page 86 This was an unfinished wood cabinet so the painting was easy, with only a little sanding needed to prep it. The painted areas were all given two coats of acrylic craft paint, left to dry well, and then sanded for an old, distressed look. The cabinet was then spattered with black paint.

I antiqued the cabinet with an oil-base antiquing medium, let it dry overnight, and then sprayed it well with a matte varnish.

I used Plaid FolkArt Acrylic craft paint in Tapioca, Hauser Dark Green, Raspberry Wine, Licorice, and Turners Yellow.

RECYCLING CAN
By Jackie Saling

Page 87 To make a recycling can like the one in Debbie's office building, wipe a new galvanized garbage can with vinegar to etch the surface; dry well. Spray with a few coats of flat off-white primer.

Sponge the can with a double-load mixture on your sponge of Tapioca and Teddy Bear Tan. I applied the designs with shapes I cut from Miracle Sponge. The sunflower on the lid and the bees around the edge were hand-painted. I hand-painted the checks but they could be sponged on.

I used Plaid FolkArt Acrylic craft paint. For the hearts: Raspberry Wine; the checks, sunflower centers, and bee details: Licorice; the sunflower spots: Tapioca; the bees and sunflower petals: Turners Yellow; line work and shading on the sunflower: Teddy Bear Tan.

FRAMES
By Jackie Saling

Page 84 The picture frames were all unfinished wood. I painted in colors that coordinate with the prints, and then sanded for a distressed look. I chose an element in the print to duplicate on the frame—a checked border, a bird, or maybe a sunflower. I then spattered the frame and applied an antiquing medium.

I like to cover the mats in matching fabric, and use a mix of fabric stiffener and water to apply the fabric to the mat board. I then have the mat cut to fit the print.

WOOD GRAINING

Materials

- Durable Colors™ for base painting
- Neutral Wall Glaze #53551
- Decorator Glaze for tinting Neutral Wall Glaze
- Wood Grainer #30114 to create wood-grain finish
- French brush #30122 for applying second base-paint color for wood graining
- Flogger brush #30115 for softening
- Brush or Glaze Roller #30118 for applying glaze
- Damp cloth rag

Wood graining is a technique that involves applying colored glaze to a base-painted surface and using a tool, such as a wood grainer, to remove the glaze and create patterns.

Instructions

1. Apply the base-paint color. Apply a second base-paint color over the first, randomly stroking the color on the surface with a French brush in the direction you're planning to create the wood grain. Let dry.

2. Brush or roll the glaze mixture onto the surface, working one area at a time.

3. While the glaze is still wet, pull the wood grainer through the glaze, rocking the tool as you pull. Your grain will look better if you pull and rock the entire length of your area before lifting the tool. Periodically wipe the excess glaze from the wood grainer with a damp cloth rag.

4. While the glaze is still wet, use the flogging brush to tap the surface to soften the lines, and to add fine detail lines that look like grain. Don't over-work the glaze.

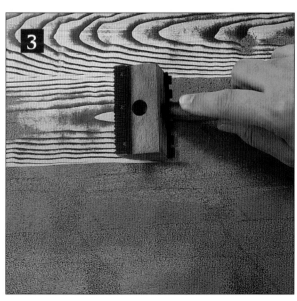

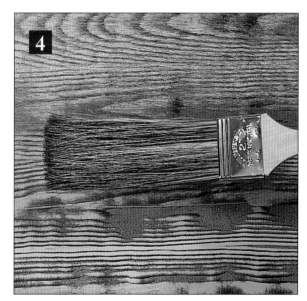

FAUX SKY

Materials

- Wall Paint: Light Blue
- Decorator Glaze™
  Neutral Wall Glaze,
  48 oz. #53551
  Linen White, 8oz.
  #53505
  Sunflower, 2 oz. #53008
  Baby Pink, 2 oz. #53015
- Stippler Brush #30128
- French Brush #30122
- Damp cloth rag

Stippling can be used to create the open and airy look of clouds and sky. First a light blue base is applied. Then, soft pastel tints are gently tapped onto the surface.

Instructions

1. Paint the ceiling with one to three coats of light blue paint; let dry between coats. Let the final coat dry about 24–36 hours.

2. Tape the moldings with long-mask masking tape.

3. Mix equal amounts of Neutral Wall Glaze and Linen White Glaze. In separate containers, mix Sunflower Glaze and Baby Pink Glaze with equal amounts of Neutral Wall Glaze.

4. Dip the bristle tips of the stippler brush into the glaze mixture. Pounce the brush on a clean disposable plate or paint tray grid to work the glaze into the brush.

5. Pounce the brush on the surface, creating drifts of white couds. Periodically wipe the brush on a damp rag to prevent glaze buildup. Reload brush as needed.

6. With the edge of the French brush, work in pink and yellow tones ever so lightly to create details and shadows of the clouds. Let dry. Remove tape.

BRICK TECHNIQUE

Brick walls can be created by taping with grout tape and sponging, stenciling, or sponge stamping. The look of brick is beautiful for walls and other surfaces.

Materials
- Base Paint: Durable Colors™ Pediment #53322
- Paints for Stippling: Black #53328 Oxblood #53310 Mojave Sunset #53306
- French Brush #30122 OR Stippler Brush #30128
- Ocean Sponge #30150
- Spray bottle
- Cloth rags

Instructions

For a weathered look, lightly mist the surface with water. Moisten a sponge and dip lightly in mortar color. Pounce sponge to distribute color, then pounce color sparingly on surface. For a mossy look, use the 'weathered look' technique with green paint. Sponge bricks before or after grout tape is removed.

1. Base-paint surface; let dry completely. Lightly mark a grid for placing the bricks on the surface, making 2¼ x 7¾ -inch bricks. Use a plumb line and a level to be sure lines are level and straight. If painting a floor, use a chalk line to mark straight lines. Tape off mortar lines with grout tape.

2. Load stippler brush or French brush with one of the stippling colors. Pounce bristles to distribute paint. Stipple the surface.

3. Stipple next color or colors, placing colors randomly for a natural look. Wipe the brush bristles on a damp cloth when changing colors to avoid mixing the paints and getting a muddy look. Let dry. Remove tape.

FLOOR CLOTH

Materials

- Decorator Products™ Durable Colors™:
  Limestone #53321
  Black #53328
  Caramel #53324
  Espresso Bean #53327
- Stamp Decor™ stamps of your choice
- Stamp Glaze Applicator #53477
- Vinyl flooring remnant
- Decorator Glaze®: Neutral #53001
- French Brush #30122
- Spatter Tool #30121
- Spray bottle filled with water

NOTE: The colors indicated above create a light colored surface to stamp or paint on. To create a floorcloth resembling Debbie's, right, adjust the paint colors and use stamps, stencils, and freehand painting for the designs.

Decorate a vinyl remnant with paint and stamps for a durable floor cloth. A pre-primed or gessoed canvas can be used as well for similar results.

Instructions

1. Prepare vinyl remnant by simply turning it to the back side. You will use this side for the decorating. Be sure the surface is clean and free of dirt. Wash if necessary. Allow to dry thoroughly. Sand surface; basecoat with Limestone. Let dry.

3. Mix Limestone, Caramel, and Espresso Bean in separate containers with Neutral glaze. Dip the tips of the French brush into the Limestone mixture and stroke and brush this lightly on the entire surface.

4. Dip the bristles of the French brush into the Caramel mixture. While the Limestone paint is still wet, pounce the surface with streaks of Caramel. Make sure to always work the pattern in a linear way.

5. Clean the bristles by wiping them on a damp cloth. Mist the surface with water from the spray bottle to keep the surface moist. Dip the French brush into the Espresso Bean mixture and pounce and brush light streaks of paint.

6. Spatter the surface lightly with Espresso Bean that has been diluted with water. Let dry completely.

8. Stamp a design onto the dry floor cloth using colors of your choice.

MOPPED GLAZE OVER STUCCO

Create a truly dramatic wall when you mop bronze glaze over a stucco wall. The mopping mitt adds a wonderful texture. If you have smooth walls, just dab on the glaze.

Materials
- Wall paint, flat or eggshell
- Decorator Glaze®: Neutral Wall Glaze, 48 oz. #53551 Olde World Bronze, 2 oz. #30107
- Decorator Tools® Mopping Mitt #30107
- Masking tape

Instructions

1. Make sure your stucco wall is clean and dry. Paint the wall with a base-paint in a color of your choice. Let dry thoroughly.

3. Tape around moldings and cabinets to protect them from the glazing.

4. Mix Olde World Bronze glaze with one tub of Neutral Wall Glaze, following package instructions.

5. Using the mopping mitt, mop the walls with Olde World Bronze glaze mixture. Use a sweeping motion to apply the glaze mixture to the stucco wall, working the glaze into the crevices and rubbing it off the smooth areas. (The smooth areas will appear to be washed with the color.) Repeat to complete the wall.

MARBLE COLUMNS

Materials

- Light taupe satin latex paint
- Decorator Glaze: Neutral, 8 oz. #53004
  Olde World Bronze, 2 oz. #53004
  Moss Green, 2 oz. #53043
  Bark Brown, 2 oz. #53033
- Decorator Tools™: French Brush #30122
  Ocean Sponge #31050
  Feathers for Detailing and Marbleizing #30101
- FolkArt® Acrylic Color: Licorice #938 OR Plaid® Faux Finish Marbleizing Kit: Black Onyx #30055
- Decorator Glaze Gloss Sealer
- Masking tape (easy mask, low tack type)
- Typing paper
- Clean dry or damp cloth
- Disposable plates
- Foam brushes
- Water and bowl

You can create the look of marble on a variety of surfaces. Here, the instructions show you how to marble a column, similar to the ones in Debbie's bedroom.

Setting Up

1. Sand surface smooth. Base-paint with two to three coats of light taupe paint. Let dry and sand between coats.

2. Mix glazes: Mix 2 oz. Olde World Bronze with 2 oz. Neutral Glaze for mixture #1; mix 1 oz. Moss Green with 2 oz. Neutral Glaze for mixture #2; for veining mixture #3, add one to two drops Bark Brown to ½ oz. of mixture #2 to deepen the color.

3. Paint the base and any bands on the column with Licorice. Let dry. Mask off black areas to shield them from marbleizing.

Instructions

1. Tear typing paper into pieces of different shapes and sizes (1–3") with rough, jagged edges. Place the torn pieces in water and wet thoroughly. While still wet, place them randomly on the column surface. The moisture will temporarily hold them in place.

2. Pour some glaze mixture #1 on a disposable plate; smooth out to a thin layer. Moisten the ocean sponge; squeeze out excess water. Dip sponge in glaze. Sponge the column randomly, patting and rubbing the glaze over the surface. Leave some areas almost free of color.

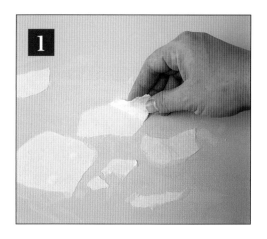

3. Pour some glaze mixture #2 on a disposable plate. Dip the tips of the bristles of the French brush in the glaze. Pounce the glaze on the column, hitting the surface hard enough to separate the bristles. Pounce glaze over some areas that were already sponged or rubbed.

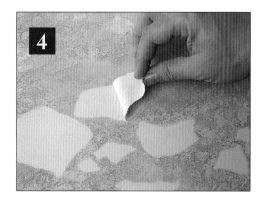

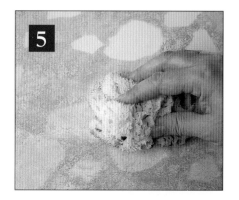

4. Remove the paper pieces from the painted surface.

5. Use the ocean sponge and/or the French brush to dab, rub, and pounce glaze mixtures #1 and #2 over the places where the paper pieces were.

6. Pour 1 teaspoon of glaze mixture #3 on a disposable plate. Add a few

drops of water and mix well. Pull the tip of the feather through the mixture. Pull the feather over the marbleized surface to create veins.

7. Option: Use a Black Onyx Kit to marbleize the column base and band. Let dry.

8. Seal with Gloss Sealer.

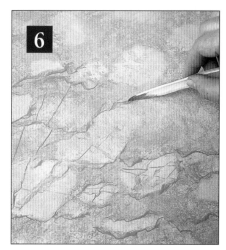

DISTRESSED FINISHES

Materials

- Durable Colors™ for base painting
- Distressing Tool Set #53475
- Decorator Glaze + Neutral Glaze, to make antiquing mediums and for spattering
- Cellulose sponge, for applying antiquing
- Sandpaper, 220 grit, for sanding surfaces

A distressed finish exhibits a comfortably worn look. Antiquing further mellows the end result. Spattering adds color and additional interest to a distressed surface.

Instructions

1. Apply wax to the surface with the grain of the wood, concentrating the wax in areas where paint would most likely be worn away by handling, such as edges.

2. Apply one to three coats of base paint color. Let dry between coats but do not sand between coats.

3. Scrape the surfaces with the smooth side of the distressing tool, working in the direction of the wood grain—in waxed areas, paint will flake off easily. Brush away the paint particles as you scrape.

4. Sand the surface to smooth the areas where paint has been removed. Optional: Use the toothy side of the distressing tool to further age the surface, creating dings, worm holes, and dents. Remove any loose particles and sand again.

5. Optional: Mix equal amounts of Bark Brown and Neutral glazes. Rub over the surface. Antiquing the distressed surface gives the paint a faded appearance and ages the wood that shows under the paint.

6. Optional: Spatter the surface with an additional color or colors.

HOW TO SPATTER

Mix a small amount of glaze mixture with water, adding water one drop at a time until the mixture is thin enough to spatter through the screen of the spatter tool. Hold the screen in one hand, pointing it toward the area to be spattered. Dip the brush in the mixture and run the bristles over the screen, flicking the paint onto the surface.

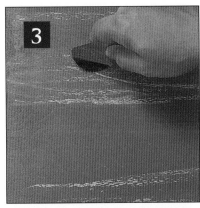

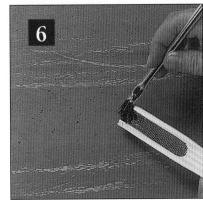

OTHER DISTRESSED EFFECTS

For a layered effect, use two or more paint colors. Allow paint to dry between colors and rub the wax stick over the painted surface before adding the next color. When all paint colors are applied and dry and the surface is scraped, the layers of paint will be exposed.

For surfaces other than wood, or if you don't want the wood to show, base paint the surface, then apply the wax and a second coat of paint. When scraping, you'll expose the first paint color, not the bare wood. This technique can be used to distress terra-cotta, plaster, papier-mâché, gypsum wall board, and concrete.

HELPFUL HINTS

The size of the spatters is determined by the consistency of the paint and how briskly the brush flicks across the spatter tool. Thinner paint makes smaller spatters.

Be sure to turn the handle of the spatter tool repeatedly while holding so paint won't build up on the back side and drip on the surface. Periodically press the spatter tool on a damp cloth and wipe the bristles of the brush to remove paint buildup.

For a diffused, hazy look, mist the surface lightly with water from a spray bottle, then spatter. The water will further dilute the paint.

CRACKLE FINISH

Materials

- Durable Colors™, used as base paint for one- and two-color crackle and as topcoat for two-color crackle
- Waterbase Varnish, as topcoat for one-color crackle
- Antiquing (Decorator Glaze + Neutral Wall Glaze), for rubbing in cracks (necessary for one-color crackle and optional for two-color crackle)
- Decorator Crackle Medium
- Foam brushes, for applying paint and crackle medium
- Cellulose sponge, for applying antiquing

What normally takes years of wind and weather can be created instantly on painted surfaces using crackle medium. The finish can be achieved with one or two colors.

Instructions

TWO-COLOR CRACKLE

1. Brush crackle medium over base-painted surface, photo 1. Let dry. When the Crackle Medium is dry, there should be an overall sheen to the surface. If any areas appear dull, apply another coat of crackle medium. Let dry.

2. Brush on an even, smooth coat of the topcoat (a second paint color), photo 2. Cracks will form. Do not overbrush—it will make the cracks disappear.

ONE-COLOR CRACKLE

1. Brush crackle medium over base-painted surface. Let dry. When the crackle medium is dry, there should be an overall sheen to the surface. If any areas appear dull, apply another coat of crackle medium. Let dry.

2. Brush on an even, smooth coat of waterbase varnish, working quickly. Cracks will form. Do not overbrush —it will make the cracks disappear. Let dry 24–36 hours.

3. To make the cracks show, you will need to apply an antiquing glaze. Mix Decorator Glaze color with Neutral Glaze to form a tinted glaze for antiquing. Apply antiquing, rubbing the antiquing in the cracks with a damp cellulose sponge. Let dry.

Practice on small projects before tackling a larger project, such as a wall.

When you begin to apply the topcoat, be sure everything is ready and use a container for the topcoat large enough to hold all the paint or varnish you need. (You won't have time to refill.)

Use a lamp to illuminate the surface so it's easier to see where you've brushed.

Apply enough of the topcoat—you can't go back and add more.

Keep a wet edge when applying the topcoat so each stroke blends with the next stroke.

In general, a thicker topcoat creates bigger cracks; a thinner topcoat creates finer, smaller cracks. You can apply a thicker topcoat to horizontal surfaces; on a vertical surface, a thick topcoat can sag. When working on a piece of furniture, turn the piece, and work one side at a time.

You can use a painting pad to apply the topcoat to large areas, such as walls. Practice first on a piece of poster board.

One-color crackle is an excellent technique for creating an aged look over surfaces that are stenciled, stamped, block printed, or painted with designs. Allow to dry, then apply crackle medium, then the waterbase varnish.

A crusted crackle finish has a more primitive, aged look. While the topcoat is still wet, use a bristle brush to lightly stroke random areas. This brushing will cause the surface to display a rough and crusty finish.

MARBLEIZING

Materials

- Durable Colors™ for base painting
- Decorator Glaze, for color layering
- Neutral wall Glaze, for mixing with Decorator Glaze
- Stippler Brush #30128
- Marbleizing Starter Set #30102 (a sponge and a feather)
- Spatter Tool #30121
- French Brush #30122
- Spray Bottle

Faux marble can be realistic—just like the real thing—or free-form and fanciful. The key to a beautiful faux marble finish is to remember that marble is irregular.

Instructions

1. Base-paint with White. Let dry. Pounce Linen White over the surface, using the stippler brush. Some areas should be heavier than others.

2. Using the stippler brush, pounce drifts of Mushroom/Bark Brown glaze mixture onto the surface. Pounce white glaze mixture randomly, using the stippler brush and the French brush.

3. Dilute 1–2 teaspoons of the white glaze mixture with water in a clean container. Using the feather, create some veins.

4. Use the tip of the feather to create cracks, dipping it in the white glaze mixture. Mist surface with water. Lightly spatter with the Mushroom/Bark Brown glaze mixture.

HELPFUL HINTS

Practice on a piece of poster board before working on your surface.

Allow some drifts and veins to fade out and disappear completely for a more authentic look.

To make veins, hold the feather the way a violinst holds a bow; drag the feather over the surface. At times wiggle the feather, or shake your hand.

Most marble patterns have cracks created by shifts in the earth that bonded again under pressure. Be sure your cracks are irregular.

Run some cracks in the direction of the drifts and veins, make others perpendicular to them. Allow a few cracks to be more vivid than others.

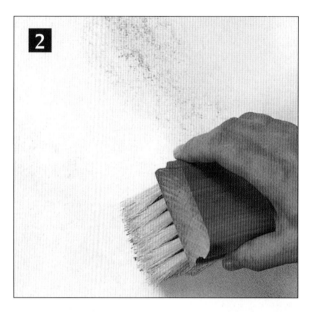

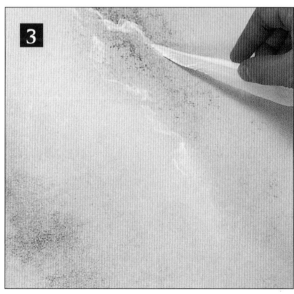

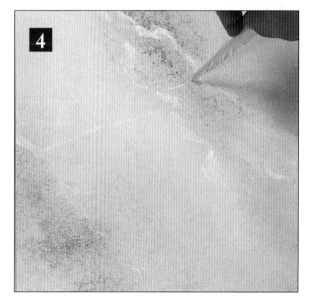

ACKNOWLEDGEMENTS

All of my staff at Mumm's The Word are always such a wonderful support to me. MTW staff that helped me create this book are Kelly Fisher, Jodi Gosse, Lou McKee, Steve Morehouse, Steve Mumm, Roberta Rose-Knauth, Jackie Saling, and Marcia Smith.

A very special thank you to the gifted artisans and seamstresses who worked on projects for my home: Nancy Eubanks, Lynn Guier, Nancy Kirkland, Bill Mound, Stephanie Puddy, Sandy Schreuer, Melcina Seibert, Jane Shawen, Margaret Sindelar, and Retta Warehime.

Also thank you to the enthusiastic and talented team at Landauer Corporation and to Nancy Martin for this great opportunity. It's been a fun project!

Debbie Mumm

RESOURCES

MUMM'S THE WORD, INC.

1116 E. Westview Ct.
Spokane, WA 99218-1384
509-466-3572
Fax 509-466-6919
http://www.DebbieMumm.com
To obtain a Mumm's The Word
catalog call 888-819-2923

PHOTOGRAPHY

All photography by Craig
Anderson and Amy Cooper
except:
Portrait of Lynn Guier on page 90
by Dan Cooley;
Portrait of Murphy Mumm on
page 68 by Barros & Barros

ARTISANS

MUMM'S THE WORD, INC.
Debbie Mumm and Jackie Saling
1116 E. Westview Ct.
Spokane, WA 99218-1384
509-466-3572
Fax 509-466-6919

LYNN GUIER DESIGNS
Lynn Guier and Bill Mound
371 Hoodoo Mountain Rd.
Priest River, ID 83856
208-265-4500

Nancy Eubanks
5915 S. Regal
Spokane, WA 99223
509-448-3052

Stephanie Puddy
509-838-5867
Fax 509-747-6328

PLAID ENTERPRISES, INC.

All decorative-painting
instructions on pages 108–121
are exerpted from the following
Plaid books:
#9277 *Decorator Glazes and
Tools—Decorator Walls* by Susan
Goans Diggers (Mopped Glaze
over Stucco)

#9401 *Techniques for Wall
Finishes* by Susan Goans Diggers
(Faux Sky)

#9348 *Decorative Finishes for
Walls and Furniture* by Susan
Goans Diggers (Marbleized
Column)

#9402 *Recipes for Faux Finishes* by
Susan Goans Diggers (Crackle
Finish; Distressed Finishes;
Marbleizing; Wood Graining)

#9415 *Durable Colors™—Inside
& Outside Decorating* by Susan
Goans Diggers (Floor Cloth)

To find out where to buy these
books contact:
PLAID ENTERPRISES, INC.
PO Box 7600
Norcross, GA 30091-7600

SOURCES FOR LICENCED PRODUCTS FROM MUMM'S THE WORD

Look for Mumm's The Word crafts, home, and decorating products in your local crafts, stationery, gifts, or housewares shop. If you cannot find what you're looking for, call the Customer Service Department of any company listed below.

FOLK ART CHARM PINS
ARRIAGA DESIGNS
810 Gail Drive
Weatherford, TX 76086
(817) 598-0415
Fax (817) 599-4818

THROWS, PILLOWS, AND FOOTSTOOLS
SIMPLY COUNTRY
P.O. Drawer 656
Wytheville, VA 24382
(800) 537-8911
Fax (540) 228-4766

CALENDARS, CHRISTMAS CARDS, NOTECARDS, STATIONERY IN A TIN, & MAGNETS
AMCAL
2500 Bisso Lane, Building 500
Concord CA 94520-4845
(800) 824-5879
Fax (510) 689-0108

QUILTING AND HOME-DEC FABRIC
SOUTH SEA IMPORTS
550 W. Artesia Blvd.
Compton, CA 90220
(800) 829-0066
Fax (310) 763-4777

CROSS-STITCH AND NEEDLEWORK KITS
DIMENSIONS
641 McKnight Street
Reading, PA 19601
(800) 523-8452
Fax (610) 372-0426

ORNAMENTS, DRAWER PULLS, COASTERS, TRAYS, MEMO CUBES, AND TRINKET BOXES
CREATIVE IMAGINATIONS
10879 Suite B. Portal Drive
Los Alamitos, CA 90720
(714) 995-2266
Fax (714) 995-3213

CERAMIC BUTTONS AND PINS
GAY BOWLES SALES, INC.
Mill Hill
PO Box 1060
Janesville WI 53547-1060
(800) 447-1332
Fax (608) 754-0665

FRAMED WATERCOLOR PRINTS
ACCENT NORTHWEST
13300 SE 30th Suite 102
Bellevue WA 98005
(800) 497-9521
Fax (425) 401-6402

UNFRAMED WATERCOLOR PRINTS AND POSTERS
WILD APPLE GRAPHICS
RR2, Route 4 West
Woodstock, VT 05091
(800) 756-8359
Fax (802) 457-3214

TILE COASTERS AND MAGNETS
HIGHLAND GRAPHICS, INC.
PO Box 1183
Springfield, TN 37172
(800) 218-7491
(817) 382-7448

FABRIC-COVERED BOXES, JOURNALS, CLOCKS, FRAMES, AND ORGANIZERS
TREND MARKETING
PO Box 5473
Chula Vista, CA 91912-5473
(800) 468-7363
Fax (619) 585-0505

RUBBER ART STAMPS
STAMPINGTON & COMPANY
22992 Mill Creek, Suites B & C
Laguna Hills, CA 92653
(714) 380-7318
Fax (714) 380-9355

SWITCHPLATE COVERS
A SWITCH IN ART
PO Box 246
Monmouth Beach, NJ 07750
(800) 626-2742
Fax (888) 517-2479

PADDED IRONING BOARD COVERS
ELCO HOME FASHIONS
690 Rennie St.
Hamilton ONT L8H3R2
(800) 462-0522
Fax (905) 547-0035

Select Publications from Martingale & Co.

Holiday Quilts and Crafts
Appliquilt® for Christmas • Tonee White
Coxcomb Quilt • Donna Hanson Eines
Easy Seasonal Wall Quilts • Deborah J. Moffett-Hall
Folded Fabric Fun • Nancy J. Martin
Quick-Sew Celebrations
Quilted for Christmas
Quilted for Christmas, Book II
Quilted for Christmas, Book III
Quilted for Christmas, Book IV
Welcome to the North Pole • Piece O' Cake
   Designs, Inc.

Home Decorating
Decorate with Quilts & Collections
   • Nancy J. Martin
The Home Decorator's Stamping Book
   • Linda Barker
Living with Little Quilts • Alice Berg,
   Mary Ellen Von Holt & Sylvia Johnson
Make Room for Quilts • Nancy J. Martin
Soft Furnishings for Your Home
   • Sharyn Skrabanich
Welcome Home™: Debbie Mumm

Stitchery/Needle Arts
Baltimore Bouquets • Mimi Dietrich
Crazy but Piecable • Hollie A. Milne
Hand-Stitched Samplers from I Done My Best
   • Saundra White
Machine Needlelace • Judy Simmons
Miniature Baltimore Album Quilts
   • Jenifer Buechel
A Passion for Ribbonry • Camela Nitschke
A Silk-Ribbon Album • Jenifer Buechel
Victorian Elegance • Lezette Thomason

Wearables
Crazy Rags • Deborah Brunner
Dress Daze • Judy Murrah
Dressed by the Best
Easy Reversible Vests • Carol Doak
Jacket Jazz • Judy Murrah
Jacket Jazz Encore • Judy Murrah
More Jazz from Judy Murrah
Quick-Sew Fleece
Sew a Work of Art Inside and Out
   • Charlotte Bird
Variations in Chenille • Nanette Holmberg

Many of these books are available at your local fabric, quilt, or craft shop. For more information, call, write, fax, or e-mail for a free color catalog.

Martingale & Company
PO Box 118
Bothell, WA 98041-0118 USA

Toll-free: 1-800-426-3126
Int'l: 425-483-3313
24-Hour Fax: 425-486-7596
E-mail: info@patchwork.com
Web: www.patchwork.com